K. CONNORS

Do it yourself home improvement

Expert Tips, Step-by-Step Projects, and Budget-Friendly Renovation Ideas for Every Homeowner

Copyright © 2024 by K. Connors

All rights reserved. No part of this publication may be reproduced, stored or transmitted in any form or by any means, electronic, mechanical, photocopying, recording, scanning, or otherwise without written permission from the publisher. It is illegal to copy this book, post it to a website, or distribute it by any other means without permission.

First edition

This book was professionally typeset on Reedsy. Find out more at reedsy.com

Contents

Introduction	1
Chapter 1: Getting Started with DIY Home Improvement	6
Chapter 2: Painting and Wallpapering	11
Chapter 3: Flooring	16
Chapter 4: Kitchen Remodeling	21
Chapter 5: Bathroom Upgrades	26
Chapter 6: Outdoor Improvements	31
Chapter 7: Energy Efficiency and Insulation	37
Chapter 8: Electrical and Lighting Projects	43
Chapter 9: Furniture and Woodworking	49
Chapter 10: Home Maintenance and Repairs	53
Conclusion	58

Introduction

Welcome to the world of DIY home improvement, where your home becomes your canvas and you, the artist, wield the tools of transformation. This book is your guide to unlocking the potential of your living space, one project at a time. Whether you're a novice just getting your feet wet or a seasoned DIY enthusiast looking to refine your skills, this journey is about turning ideas into reality and making your home uniquely yours.

So, why embark on this DIY adventure? For starters, there's the undeniable satisfaction of completing a project with your own two hands. It's the joy of standing back and admiring a freshly painted room or a newly installed set of shelves and knowing you did that. Plus, there's the potential for significant cost savings. Hiring professionals can be expensive, and while there are certainly projects that require expert hands, many tasks around the home are well within the grasp of a determined DIYer.

But beyond the practical benefits, there's a deeper, more personal reason to take on home improvement projects yourself. It's about making your living space reflect who you are. Every project you undertake adds a bit of your personality to your home, whether it's a bold accent wall in the living room or a custom-built bookshelf in the study. Your home becomes a narrative of your creativity, a place that tells your story in every corner.

Now, before we dive into the nuts and bolts of DIY, let's talk about who this book is for. Are you a first-time homeowner feeling a bit overwhelmed by the prospect of maintenance and improvement? Maybe you're someone who's always enjoyed tinkering but isn't sure where to start on bigger projects. Or perhaps you're an experienced DIYer looking for fresh ideas and tips to take your skills to the next level. No matter where you fall on this spectrum, this book is designed to guide you through the process with clear instructions, practical advice, and a dash of humor to keep things light.

Using this book is straightforward. Each chapter focuses on a different aspect of home improvement, from painting and wallpapering to more complex tasks like electrical work and custom furniture building. We'll start with the basics, covering the essential tools and materials you'll need, and then move on to planning and preparation, because as any seasoned DIYer will tell you, half the battle is in the planning. Each project is broken down into manageable steps, with plenty of tips and tricks to help you avoid common pitfalls.

Safety is paramount in any DIY endeavor, and this book places a strong emphasis on it. We'll cover the importance of protective gear, safe handling of tools and materials, and how to identify when a project might be best left to the professionals. Remember, the goal is to improve your home, not to end up in the emergency room.

One of the first things to get a handle on is your tool kit. Think of it as your artist's palette. A well-stocked tool kit is essential for any home improvement project, and while you don't need to buy out the entire hardware store, there are a few basics you shouldn't be without. A good quality hammer, a set of screwdrivers, pliers, a tape measure, and a utility knife are the foundation. From there, you can expand to include power tools like a cordless drill, a circular saw, and a sander, depending on the projects you plan to tackle.

Materials are the next consideration. Knowing what you'll need for a project and having it on hand can save you countless trips to the store. This book includes comprehensive lists of materials for each project, along with tips

INTRODUCTION

on selecting the right products. For example, when it comes to paint, there's a dizzying array of options, from finishes to colors to eco-friendly choices. We'll help you navigate these decisions so you can pick the best materials for your project.

Planning and preparation are often the unsung heroes of a successful DIY project. It's tempting to dive right in, but taking the time to plan your project can make a world of difference. This means measuring your space accurately, drawing up a detailed plan, and scheduling your work in stages. Good preparation helps you anticipate challenges and ensures you have everything you need before you start, which can save a lot of frustration down the line.

As we journey through the chapters, you'll find that each project builds on the skills and knowledge you've gained. We'll start with relatively simple tasks like painting and wallpapering, which are great for beginners and can dramatically change the look of a room. You'll learn how to choose the right paint, prepare your surfaces, and apply various techniques to achieve professional-looking results. Wallpapering might seem daunting, but with the right guidance, it can be a rewarding way to add texture and personality to your walls.

From there, we'll move on to flooring. Whether you're interested in installing hardwood, laminate, or tile, this chapter covers the pros and cons of each option and provides step-by-step instructions for installation. You'll learn how to prepare your subfloor, lay your materials, and finish the job with finesse. Flooring projects can be physically demanding, but they're incredibly satisfying and can add significant value to your home.

The kitchen and bathroom are two areas where DIY improvements can have a major impact. In the kitchen, we'll guide you through planning a remodel, from designing your layout to installing cabinets and countertops. You'll also learn how to update appliances and fixtures to create a space that's both functional and beautiful. In the bathroom, we'll cover everything from refreshing the decor with new tiles and fixtures to tackling more complex plumbing tasks.

Outdoor improvements are another exciting aspect of DIY home improvement. Whether you have a sprawling garden or a compact patio, there are countless ways to enhance your outdoor space. We'll explore garden design, deck and patio construction, and even outdoor lighting and decor projects that can transform your yard into an inviting oasis.

Energy efficiency and insulation are hot topics in the home improvement world, and for good reason. Improving your home's insulation can reduce energy costs and make your living space more comfortable. This chapter will guide you through different types of insulation, from traditional fiberglass to modern spray foam, and provide tips on installation. We'll also look at energy-efficient windows and doors, and even delve into renewable energy options like solar panels and wind turbines.

Electrical projects can be intimidating, but they don't have to be. With the right knowledge and precautions, many basic electrical tasks are well within the reach of a DIYer. We'll cover essential safety tips, tools, and techniques for tasks like installing light fixtures and setting up smart home devices. By the end of this chapter, you'll have the confidence to tackle these projects safely and effectively.

Woodworking and furniture building are where you can really let your creativity shine. Whether you're building a simple shelf or a custom piece of furniture, this chapter will guide you through the basics of woodworking. You'll learn about different types of wood, essential tools, and finishing techniques. We'll also explore refinishing and upcycling old furniture to give it new life, as well as creating custom built-ins and storage solutions that maximize your space.

Finally, no home improvement guide would be complete without addressing maintenance and repairs. Regular maintenance is key to keeping your home in

INTRODUCTION

good condition and preventing minor issues from becoming major problems. This chapter provides seasonal checklists, tips for routine maintenance tasks, and step-by-step guides for common repairs. We'll also cover how to handle emergency repairs and what tools and materials you should always have on hand.

In essence, this book is about empowerment. It's about giving you the knowledge and confidence to take control of your living space and make it truly your own. Whether you're fixing a leaky faucet or building a new deck, each project is a step towards creating a home that reflects your style, meets your needs, and brings you joy. So grab your tools, roll up your sleeves, and let's get started on this exciting DIY adventure together.

Chapter 1: Getting Started with DIY Home Improvement

So, you've decided to dive into the world of DIY home improvement. Fantastic! Whether you're aiming to fix that pesky leaky faucet, paint your living room a fresh new color, or take on a more ambitious project like building a deck, you're in for an exciting and rewarding journey. But before you jump in headfirst, it's important to lay a solid foundation. This chapter is all about getting you started on the right foot.

First things first: assessing your home improvement needs. Take a good, long look around your home. What bothers you the most? Is it that outdated kitchen that looks like it hasn't been touched since the 80s? Or maybe it's the lack of storage space that's driving you up the wall. Whatever it is, make a list. Prioritize the projects based on urgency and impact. This will not only help you stay organized but also ensure that you tackle the most important tasks first.

Once you've got your list, it's time to set some realistic goals and budgets. It's easy to get carried away with grand plans of a complete home makeover, but remember, Rome wasn't built in a day. Start with small, manageable projects and work your way up. This way, you'll gain confidence and skills as you go. When setting your budget, be realistic about what you can afford. Factor in the cost of materials, tools, and any additional expenses that might crop up. And always, always have a contingency fund. Trust me, there will be unexpected costs.

Speaking of tools and materials, let's talk about the basics you'll need to get started. Think of your tools as your best friends in the world of DIY. A good quality hammer, a set of screwdrivers (both flathead and Phillips), pliers, a tape measure, and a utility knife are your essentials. These are the bread and butter of any tool kit. From there, you can expand your collection based on the projects you plan to tackle. For instance, a cordless drill is a lifesaver for most tasks, and a circular saw can be invaluable for woodworking projects.

As for materials, it's important to know what you need before you start. This can save you countless trips to the hardware store. For example, if you're planning to paint a room, you'll need not just paint but also primer, painter's tape, drop cloths, brushes, and rollers. Make a list of everything you'll need for your project and check it twice. This not only helps you stay organized but also ensures that you don't have to stop mid-project to run to the store.

Now, let's talk about planning and preparation. This might not be the most glamorous part of DIY, but it's arguably the most important. Good planning can make the difference between a smooth, successful project and a complete disaster. Start by measuring your space accurately. Whether you're hanging a picture or laying new flooring, precise measurements are crucial. Sketch out a detailed plan of your project, including dimensions and materials needed. This will serve as your roadmap and help you stay on track.

Scheduling your work in stages is another key aspect of planning. Break your project down into manageable steps and assign a timeframe for each one. This not only helps you stay organized but also prevents you from feeling overwhelmed. For instance, if you're renovating a kitchen, you might start with demolition, then move on to installing cabinets, followed by countertops, and finally, appliances and fixtures. By tackling one stage at a time, you'll make steady progress without getting bogged down.

Safety is another critical consideration in DIY. The last thing you want is to end up in the emergency room because you didn't take the necessary precautions. Always wear protective gear, such as gloves, safety goggles, and a mask, when working with hazardous materials or power tools. Make sure your workspace is well-ventilated, especially when using paints, solvents, or adhesives. And never underestimate the importance of a first aid kit. Keep one handy at all times, just in case.

Now, let's dive into some of the initial projects you can start with. Painting is a great beginner project that can have a huge impact on the look and feel of your home. Start by choosing the right paint. There are so many options out there, from matte to glossy finishes, and it can be overwhelming. For walls, a satin or eggshell finish is a good all-around choice. It's durable and easy to clean, making it ideal for high-traffic areas like kitchens and bathrooms. If you're painting trim or furniture, a semi-gloss or high-gloss finish can give a nice, polished look.

Before you start painting, prepare your surfaces. This means cleaning the walls to remove dust and grease, patching any holes or cracks, and sanding rough areas. Priming is also important, especially if you're painting over a dark color or a surface that's never been painted before. Primer helps the paint adhere better and ensures a more even finish.

When it comes to the actual painting, take your time. Use painter's tape to protect areas you don't want to paint, like trim and windows. Apply paint in thin, even coats, and let each coat dry completely before applying the next. This might seem tedious, but it's worth the effort for a professional-looking finish. And don't forget to clean your brushes and rollers thoroughly when you're done. This not only prolongs their life but also ensures they're ready for your next project.

Another great beginner project is installing shelves. This is not only functional but also a great way to add a personal touch to your space. Start by choosing the right type of shelves for your needs. Floating shelves are a popular choice for their sleek, modern look, but they require careful installation to ensure they're secure. Bracketed shelves are easier to install and can hold more weight, making them ideal for heavier items like books.

Before you start drilling holes, use a stud finder to locate the studs in your wall. Shelves need to be anchored to studs for maximum stability. If you can't find a stud where you want to place your shelf, use wall anchors to secure the screws. Measure and mark where you want your shelves to go, making sure they're level. Then, drill pilot holes for the screws, attach the brackets or mounting hardware, and finally, place your shelves.

One of the most satisfying DIY projects is tiling. Whether you're updating a kitchen backsplash or adding a new floor in your bathroom, tiles can transform a space. Start by choosing the right tiles for your project. Ceramic and porcelain tiles are durable and easy to clean, making them ideal for kitchens and bathrooms. Natural stone tiles, like marble and granite, add a touch of luxury but require more maintenance.

Before you start tiling, prepare your surface. This means cleaning it thoroughly and making sure it's flat and level. If you're tiling a floor, you might need to install a backer board to provide a stable base. Measure and mark where your tiles will go, starting from the center of the room and working your way out. This ensures that any cut tiles will be at the edges, where they're less noticeable.

When it comes to applying the tiles, use a notched trowel to spread adhesive evenly on the surface. Press each tile firmly into place, using spacers to ensure even gaps between them. Once the adhesive has dried, apply grout to the gaps, using a rubber float to press it into the spaces. Wipe off any excess grout with a damp sponge and let it cure for at least 24 hours before using the area.

As you gain confidence and skills with these smaller projects, you can start tackling more ambitious ones. Perhaps you'll build a custom piece of furniture, like a coffee table or a bookshelf. Or maybe you'll take on a full room renovation, complete with new flooring, paint, and fixtures. The possibilities are endless, and each project is an opportunity to learn and grow as a DIYer.

In conclusion, getting started with DIY home improvement is all about preparation, planning, and practice. Start small, build your skills, and gradually take on more challenging projects. Remember to prioritize safety, invest in quality tools, and enjoy the process. Your home is a reflection of you, and with each project, you're making it more uniquely yours. So roll up your sleeves, grab your tools, and get ready to transform your living space one project at a time.

Chapter 2: Painting and Wallpapering

Ah, painting and wallpapering—the bread and butter of home improvement. These projects are where you can really let your creativity shine, transforming a room from drab to fab with just a few strokes of a brush or a roll of wallpaper. But before you dip that brush into the paint can or unroll that wallpaper, let's dive into the details of how to get the best results.

Painting Basics: Choosing the right paint can feel like trying to pick the perfect wine pairing for dinner. There are so many options, and each has its own set of characteristics. Let's break it down.

When it comes to finishes, you've got flat, eggshell, satin, semi-gloss, and gloss. Flat paint has no shine and is great for hiding imperfections on walls, but it's not very washable, making it less ideal for high-traffic areas. Eggshell has a slight sheen and is more washable, making it a good middle-ground choice. Satin offers a bit more sheen and durability, making it perfect for kitchens and bathrooms. Semi-gloss and gloss are the most durable and washable, making them excellent choices for trim and doors, but they do highlight imperfections, so prep work is key.

Color selection can be overwhelming, but it's also where the fun begins. Consider the mood you want to create. Light colors can make a room feel larger and more open, while dark colors can add warmth and coziness. Don't be afraid to play with bold colors and accent walls. They can add personality and drama to a space. If you're unsure about a color, get a sample and paint a small section of your wall. Live with it for a few days and see how it looks in different lighting.

Now, let's talk about tools. A good paint job starts with good tools. Invest in high-quality brushes and rollers. Cheap tools can shed bristles and leave lint in your paint, leading to a less-than-perfect finish. You'll need a variety of brushes: a 2- to 2.5-inch angled brush for cutting in around edges, a 3- to 4-inch flat brush for larger areas, and small detail brushes for trim and corners. For rollers, choose ones with the appropriate nap length for your surface. Smooth surfaces like drywall need a short nap, while textured surfaces like stucco need a longer nap.

Preparation is key to a professional-looking paint job. Start by clearing the room of furniture and covering the floor with drop cloths. Use painter's tape to protect trim, windows, and any areas you don't want to paint. Clean the walls to remove dust and grease. A mixture of mild detergent and water works well. Fill any holes or cracks with spackle, then sand the patches smooth once they're dry. Sand any rough areas on the walls as well. Dust off the walls again after sanding.

Priming is an often-overlooked but crucial step. Primer helps paint adhere better to the surface and ensures a more even finish. It's especially important if you're painting over a dark color, a glossy finish, or a surface that's never been painted before. Choose a primer that's appropriate for your surface and the type of paint you're using. Apply the primer with a brush and roller, just as you would with paint, and let it dry completely.

When you're ready to paint, start with the edges and corners, using your angled brush to cut in. This means painting a few inches out from the edges, creating a border that you'll fill in with your roller. Cutting in can be tedious, but it's important for getting a clean line between the walls and trim. Once you've cut in, use a roller to fill in the larger areas. Work in sections, starting from

CHAPTER 2: PAINTING AND WALLPAPERING

the top of the wall and working your way down. Use long, even strokes, and overlap your passes to avoid streaks.

Applying multiple thin coats is better than one thick coat. This helps prevent drips and ensures a smooth, even finish. Let each coat dry completely before applying the next. The drying time will depend on the type of paint and the conditions in your room, so check the manufacturer's instructions.

Now, let's switch gears to wallpapering. Wallpaper can add texture, pattern, and color to a room in ways that paint simply can't. But it does require a bit more precision and patience.

Choosing the right wallpaper starts with considering the style and mood of the room. Bold patterns can make a statement and become a focal point, while subtle patterns can add depth and interest without overwhelming the space. When selecting a pattern, think about the scale. Large patterns can make a small room feel even smaller, while small patterns can get lost in a large room. Balance is key.

Before you start wallpapering, you'll need to gather your tools: a wallpaper smoother, a sharp utility knife, a tape measure, a level, a plumb line, a wallpaper brush or roller, and a seam roller. You'll also need wallpaper paste if your wallpaper isn't pre-pasted.

Preparation is crucial here as well. Remove any old wallpaper first. If it's stubborn, use a wallpaper steamer or a mixture of water and vinegar to help loosen it. Once the old wallpaper is removed, clean the walls thoroughly to remove any residue. Repair any holes or cracks with spackle and sand them smooth. Prime the walls with a wallpaper primer to ensure the best adhesion.

When you're ready to hang your wallpaper, start by measuring and cutting your strips. Measure the height of your wall and add a few extra inches at the top and bottom for trimming. Use a sharp utility knife to cut the wallpaper. If your wallpaper has a pattern, make sure to match the pattern when cutting subsequent strips.

Use a plumb line or a level to draw a straight vertical line on the wall where you'll start hanging your first strip. This line will ensure your wallpaper is straight. Apply paste to the back of the wallpaper if it's not pre-pasted, and then fold the strip in on itself, paste side to paste side, in a process called "booking." Let it sit for a few minutes to activate the paste.

Starting at the top of the wall, align the edge of the wallpaper with your plumb line and press it onto the wall. Use a wallpaper smoother to remove any air bubbles and ensure good adhesion. Work your way down, smoothing as you go. Trim the excess at the top and bottom with your utility knife.

When hanging subsequent strips, take care to match the pattern and butt the edges together without overlapping. Use a seam roller to press the seams flat. Continue this process around the room, using the same booking and smoothing technique for each strip.

Wallpapering corners can be tricky. For inside corners, cut the wallpaper so it wraps around the corner and overlaps by about half an inch. For outside corners, wrap the wallpaper around the corner and trim it to leave a small overlap. Use your seam roller to press the edges firmly in place.

Once all your wallpaper is up, give it time to dry completely. This can take a day or two, depending on the humidity in the room. Avoid heavy cleaning or hanging anything on the walls until the wallpaper is fully set.

Both painting and wallpapering can transform a room dramatically and are within the reach of most DIY enthusiasts. The key to success lies in preparation and patience. Take your time with each step, and don't rush the process. The results will be worth it.

CHAPTER 2: PAINTING AND WALLPAPERING

In this chapter, we've covered the basics of painting and wallpapering, from selecting the right materials and tools to preparing your surfaces and applying your chosen finish. These projects are not only a great way to refresh your home but also an opportunity to express your personal style and creativity. So, roll up your sleeves, gather your supplies, and get ready to give your walls a new lease on life. With a bit of effort and attention to detail, you'll be amazed at what you can achieve.

Chapter 3: Flooring

When it comes to home improvement, few things have as immediate and dramatic an impact as updating your floors. Whether you're replacing old, worn-out carpet with sleek hardwood or adding a splash of style with new tiles, the right flooring can completely transform a room. This chapter will guide you through the ins and outs of various flooring options, from selecting materials to installation techniques. Let's get those floors looking fabulous.

First, let's talk about the different types of flooring available and their respective pros and cons. Hardwood flooring is a perennial favorite, and for good reason. It's timeless, durable, and adds warmth and elegance to any room. Hardwood can be solid or engineered. Solid hardwood is made from a single piece of wood and can be sanded and refinished multiple times, making it incredibly long-lasting. Engineered hardwood consists of a top layer of real wood veneer over layers of plywood, providing greater stability and resistance to moisture. This makes it a good choice for areas like basements where solid hardwood might warp.

Laminate flooring is another popular choice. It mimics the look of hardwood but is typically more affordable and easier to install. Laminate is composed of a photographic layer that replicates wood, stone, or tile, topped with a clear protective layer. It's highly durable and resistant to scratches and dents, making it a great option for high-traffic areas or homes with pets and kids. However, it doesn't have the same feel or longevity as real hardwood and can't be refinished if it gets damaged.

Vinyl flooring has come a long way in recent years and now offers a wide range of styles, from planks that look like wood to tiles that mimic stone. It's incredibly versatile, waterproof, and easy to maintain. Luxury vinyl plank (LVP) and luxury vinyl tile (LVT) are particularly popular for their durability and realistic appearance. Vinyl is also softer underfoot compared to wood or tile, making it more comfortable to walk on. However, it can be prone to fading over time if exposed to too much sunlight.

Tile flooring is a fantastic option for kitchens, bathrooms, and entryways due to its water resistance and durability. Ceramic and porcelain tiles are the most common types. Ceramic tiles are made from clay and are typically finished with a durable glaze. They're versatile and available in a wide range of colors, sizes, and patterns. Porcelain tiles are denser and more durable, making them suitable for high-traffic areas and even outdoor use. They're also more resistant to water and stains. Both ceramic and porcelain tiles are relatively easy to clean and maintain, though they can be cold and hard underfoot.

Carpet remains a popular choice for bedrooms and living areas, offering comfort and warmth. It's available in a variety of materials, including wool, nylon, polyester, and olefin, each with its own benefits. Wool is natural and luxurious but can be pricey. Nylon is durable and resistant to stains and wear, making it a great choice for high-traffic areas. Polyester is soft and resistant to fading but less durable than nylon. Olefin is budget-friendly and resistant to moisture, making it suitable for basements and outdoor areas.

Now that we've covered the basics of different flooring types, let's dive into the installation process. Regardless of the type of flooring you choose, proper preparation is key to a successful installation. Start by removing any existing flooring. This might involve pulling up carpet, prying up old hardwood or laminate, or chipping away at old tiles. Once the old flooring is removed, inspect the subfloor. It needs to be clean, dry, and level. Any imperfections in the subfloor can affect the installation and longevity of your new flooring.

For hardwood flooring, acclimation is an important step. This involves letting the wood sit in the room where it will be installed for several days to adjust to the room's temperature and humidity. This helps prevent the wood from expanding or contracting after installation, which can cause gaps or warping. When you're ready to install, start by laying a moisture barrier and underlayment if needed. This provides a smooth surface for the wood and helps reduce noise. Hardwood flooring is typically installed using a tongue-and-groove system, where each board locks into the next. Use a flooring nailer to secure the boards to the subfloor, making sure to leave a small gap around the edges of the room to allow for expansion.

Laminate flooring is a bit easier to install, making it a popular choice for DIYers. Like hardwood, laminate often uses a tongue-and-groove system, but the boards usually snap together without the need for nails or glue. Start by laying a moisture barrier and underlayment if necessary. Lay the first row of planks along the longest wall, using spacers to maintain a gap for expansion. Continue laying the planks row by row, snapping each one into place. Use a tapping block and mallet to ensure the joints are tight. Once all the planks are installed, remove the spacers and install baseboards to cover the gaps.

Vinyl flooring installation varies depending on the type. For peel-and-stick tiles, start by thoroughly cleaning the subfloor. Measure and mark a center point in the room, and begin laying the tiles from the center outwards. Press each tile firmly in place, making sure to align the edges. For floating vinyl planks, the installation process is similar to laminate. Lay a moisture barrier if needed, and start laying the planks from the longest wall, snapping them together as you go. Cut the planks to fit using a utility knife, scoring and snapping them for a clean edge.

Tile installation requires a bit more precision and patience. Start by laying out your tiles to determine the best placement and minimize cuts. Use a chalk line to mark a straight starting point. Apply a thin layer of thin-set mortar to a small section of the floor using a notched trowel. Press each tile firmly into the mortar, using spacers to maintain even gaps. Continue working in small sections, and periodically check that the tiles are level. Once all the tiles are laid and the mortar has set, remove the spacers and apply grout to the gaps using a rubber float. Wipe off any excess grout with a damp sponge and let it cure.

Carpet installation is a bit more involved and might require professional help, especially for large rooms. If you're up for the challenge, start by installing tack strips around the perimeter of the room. Lay down carpet padding and staple it in place. Roll out the carpet and cut it to size, leaving a few inches of excess around the edges. Use a knee kicker to stretch the carpet onto the tack strips, then trim the excess with a utility knife. Finish by tucking the edges under the baseboards.

No matter what type of flooring you choose, maintenance is key to keeping it looking its best. For hardwood floors, regular sweeping and occasional mopping with a damp (not wet) mop will keep them clean. Avoid using harsh cleaners that can strip the finish. Every few years, you might need to refinish your hardwood floors to restore their shine. For laminate and vinyl floors, sweeping and mopping with a mild cleaner is usually sufficient. Avoid using excessive water on laminate floors, as it can cause the planks to swell.

Tile floors are easy to maintain with regular sweeping and mopping. Use a mild cleaner and avoid abrasive tools that can scratch the surface. Sealing grout lines every year or so can help prevent stains and keep your tiles looking fresh. For carpet, regular vacuuming is essential to remove dirt and debris. Deep clean your carpets with a steam cleaner every year or so to remove embedded dirt and refresh the fibers. Spot clean spills immediately to prevent stains from setting.

Updating your flooring can seem like a daunting task, but with the right tools, materials, and preparation, it's a project that can be tackled by most DIY enthusiasts. The key is to take your time, follow the proper steps, and don't be afraid to ask for help if needed. The rewards are well worth the effort, as new flooring can completely transform your home, adding value, comfort, and style.

From the timeless elegance of hardwood to the versatile durability of vinyl, the right flooring can set the stage for the rest of your home's decor. Whether you're updating a single room or tackling an entire house, this chapter has covered the essentials to get you started on the right foot. So lace up those work boots, gather your tools, and get ready to roll out a beautiful new floor.

Chapter 4: Kitchen Remodeling

The kitchen is often referred to as the heart of the home. It's where meals are prepared, conversations are had, and memories are made. So, it's no wonder that kitchen remodeling is one of the most popular and rewarding home improvement projects. In this chapter, we'll delve into the world of kitchen remodeling, covering everything from planning and design to the nitty-gritty of installation and finishing touches. By the end, you'll have a comprehensive understanding of how to transform your kitchen into a functional, beautiful space that meets your needs and reflects your personal style.

Planning your kitchen remodel is the first and most crucial step. It sets the foundation for everything that follows. Start by assessing your current kitchen and identifying what works and what doesn't. Maybe you love the location of your sink but hate the lack of counter space. Or perhaps the cabinets are functional but outdated. Make a list of your priorities, focusing on both aesthetics and functionality. This will help guide your decisions throughout the remodel.

Next, set a realistic budget. Kitchen remodels can range from a few thousand dollars for minor updates to tens of thousands for a complete overhaul. Determine how much you're willing and able to spend, and allocate funds to different aspects of the project, such as cabinets, countertops, appliances, and labor. Be sure to include a contingency fund for unexpected expenses. Remodeling projects often uncover hidden issues, like outdated wiring or plumbing problems, that need to be addressed.

With your priorities and budget in place, it's time to start designing your new kitchen. Consider the layout first. The classic work triangle, which places the sink, stove, and refrigerator in a triangular arrangement, is a tried-and-true design principle that maximizes efficiency. However, modern kitchens often incorporate additional elements like islands and breakfast bars, so feel free to adapt the layout to suit your needs. Use graph paper or online design tools to sketch out different configurations until you find one that works.

When selecting materials and finishes, think about both style and durability. Cabinets are one of the most prominent features in any kitchen, so choose a style that complements your home's overall aesthetic. Shaker-style cabinets, with their clean lines and classic look, are a popular choice that works well in both traditional and contemporary kitchens. For a more modern look, consider flat-panel cabinets with a sleek, minimalist design.

Countertops are another key element. Granite and quartz are popular choices for their durability and natural beauty, but there are many other options to consider, such as marble, butcher block, and laminate. Each material has its pros and cons. Granite is heat-resistant and extremely durable but can be pricey and requires regular sealing. Quartz is non-porous and low-maintenance but can be susceptible to heat damage. Butcher block adds warmth and charm but needs regular oiling to prevent drying and cracking.

Appliances are the workhorses of your kitchen, so choose ones that fit your needs and lifestyle. Stainless steel is a timeless choice that complements most kitchen styles, but newer finishes like black stainless and slate are gaining popularity for their modern look and smudge-resistant properties. When selecting appliances, consider their energy efficiency, capacity, and features. For example, a double oven can be a game-changer for those who love to bake, while a French door refrigerator offers easy access to fresh foods.

CHAPTER 4: KITCHEN REMODELING

Lighting is an often-overlooked aspect of kitchen design but is crucial for both functionality and ambiance. A combination of task lighting, ambient lighting, and accent lighting will create a well-lit, inviting space. Under-cabinet lights provide focused illumination for tasks like chopping vegetables, while pendant lights over an island or dining area add style and ambient light. Recessed ceiling lights or a central fixture can provide general illumination for the entire room.

Once you've finalized your design, it's time to move on to the actual remodeling process. This typically begins with demolition. If you're doing a major remodel, this might involve removing old cabinets, countertops, appliances, and flooring. Be sure to turn off the power and water supply before you start. Use a hammer and pry bar to carefully remove cabinets and countertops, and a utility knife to cut through caulk and sealant. For flooring, a flooring scraper can make quick work of adhesive-backed tiles or linoleum.

With the old kitchen stripped away, you may need to address any underlying issues. This is the time to update wiring, plumbing, and insulation as needed. For electrical work, you may want to hire a licensed electrician to ensure everything is up to code and safe. If you're moving plumbing fixtures like sinks or dishwashers, consider consulting a plumber. Proper installation is crucial to avoid leaks and water damage down the road.

Next comes the installation of new elements, starting with the cabinetry. Installing cabinets can be a bit tricky, but with careful measurement and a bit of patience, it's definitely doable. Start by locating the wall studs and marking their positions on the wall. Use a level to draw a horizontal line where the top of the cabinets will go. Begin with the upper cabinets, as they're easier to install without the lower cabinets in the way. Attach a ledger board to the wall along the level line to support the cabinets during installation. Use screws to secure the cabinets to the studs, and check for level and plumb as you go.

Once the upper cabinets are in place, move on to the lower cabinets. Align them with the wall studs and secure them with screws. Use shims to level the cabinets if your floor is uneven. After the cabinets are installed, you can proceed with the countertops. If you've chosen stone countertops like granite or quartz, they'll likely be fabricated and installed by professionals. For DIY-friendly materials like laminate or butcher block, measure and cut the countertop to size, then secure it to the cabinets with screws and adhesive.

With the major elements in place, you can focus on the finishing touches. Install the backsplash, which can be both functional and decorative. Tile is a popular choice for backsplashes due to its durability and ease of cleaning. Choose a tile that complements your countertop and cabinet colors. Measure and mark the area, then apply tile adhesive with a notched trowel. Press the tiles into place, using spacers to ensure even gaps. Once the adhesive has set, apply grout to the gaps with a rubber float, and wipe off any excess with a damp sponge.

Next, install your new appliances. Carefully follow the manufacturer's instructions for each appliance, and make sure all connections are secure. If you're not comfortable with electrical or gas hookups, it's best to hire a professional to handle these tasks. Once the appliances are in place, you can install the sink and faucet. Apply plumber's putty to the base of the faucet before inserting it into the sink holes, then secure it with the mounting nuts provided. Connect the water supply lines and test for leaks.

Finally, add the finishing touches that make your kitchen uniquely yours. Install hardware like cabinet knobs and drawer pulls, which can add a touch of style and make cabinets easier to open. Choose hardware that complements your overall design, whether it's sleek and modern or classic and traditional. Add decorative elements like a stylish rug, potted plants, or artwork to bring warmth and personality to the space.

Throughout the remodeling process, keep in mind that patience and attention to detail are key. Take your time with each step, and don't rush the process. A

CHAPTER 4: KITCHEN REMODELING

well-planned and executed kitchen remodel can add significant value to your home and make it a more enjoyable place to cook, eat, and gather with family and friends. From the initial planning stages to the final finishing touches, every decision you make contributes to creating a kitchen that is both beautiful and functional.

In this chapter, we've covered the essential elements of kitchen remodeling, from planning and budgeting to selecting materials and installing new fixtures. By following these guidelines and taking the time to carefully plan and execute each step, you'll be well on your way to creating a kitchen that meets your needs and exceeds your expectations. So roll up your sleeves, grab your tools, and get ready to transform your kitchen into the heart of your home.

Chapter 5: Bathroom Upgrades

Bathrooms are small but mighty spaces that can have a significant impact on the comfort and functionality of your home. Upgrading a bathroom can range from simple cosmetic changes to complete overhauls involving plumbing and structural modifications. In this chapter, we'll explore a variety of bathroom upgrades, from budget-friendly updates to more extensive renovations. Let's dive into the world of bathroom improvements and transform these essential rooms into stylish and efficient sanctuaries.

Refreshing your bathroom can start with some straightforward and inexpensive updates that make a big difference. One of the easiest ways to breathe new life into a bathroom is by updating the fixtures. Swapping out old faucets, showerheads, and towel bars for new ones can instantly modernize the space. There are countless styles to choose from, whether you prefer sleek and modern or classic and traditional. Opt for finishes that complement your existing decor, such as brushed nickel, chrome, or matte black.

Another simple upgrade is to replace the hardware on your vanity cabinets and drawers. New knobs and pulls can give your vanity a fresh look without the need for a complete replacement. Look for hardware that matches your new fixtures for a cohesive design. If your vanity itself is looking tired, consider giving it a facelift with a fresh coat of paint. A bold color can make a statement, while a neutral tone can create a calming atmosphere.

CHAPTER 5: BATHROOM UPGRADES

Lighting is crucial in a bathroom, both for functionality and ambiance. If your bathroom lighting consists of a single overhead fixture, consider adding some task lighting around the vanity. Wall-mounted sconces or pendant lights on either side of the mirror provide even, flattering light for grooming tasks. An overhead light with a dimmer switch can create a relaxing mood for those long soaks in the tub. For a modern touch, consider installing LED strip lighting under the vanity or along the ceiling.

Mirrors are another focal point in any bathroom. If your current mirror is plain or outdated, replacing it with a stylish framed mirror can elevate the entire space. Frameless mirrors with beveled edges offer a sleek, contemporary look, while framed mirrors add a touch of elegance. For added functionality, consider a mirror with built-in LED lighting or a defogging feature, which is especially useful in small or poorly ventilated bathrooms.

Updating your bathroom's color scheme is a powerful way to transform the space. A fresh coat of paint on the walls can work wonders. Light, neutral colors like soft grays, warm beiges, or crisp whites can make a small bathroom feel more spacious and airy. If you're feeling adventurous, consider an accent wall in a bold color or even a wallpaper with a fun pattern. Just be sure to choose moisture-resistant paint or wallpaper designed for bathrooms to prevent peeling and mold growth.

One of the most impactful bathroom upgrades is new tile. Whether you're replacing the floor, the shower surround, or adding a backsplash, tile can add texture, color, and durability to your bathroom. There are countless options to choose from, including ceramic, porcelain, natural stone, and glass. Subway tiles are a classic choice that never goes out of style, while large-format tiles can make a small bathroom feel bigger by reducing the number of grout lines. Mosaic tiles can add a touch of luxury and are great for creating decorative accents.

If you're tackling a tiling project, start by planning your layout and calculating the amount of tile you'll need. Make sure to account for any pattern repeats and extra tiles for cuts and waste. Prepare your surface by ensuring it's clean, dry, and level. Use a notched trowel to apply tile adhesive evenly, and press the tiles into place, using spacers to maintain even gaps. Once the adhesive has set, apply grout to the gaps with a rubber float, and wipe off any excess with a damp sponge. Sealing the grout once it's dry will help prevent stains and moisture penetration.

Another key area to consider when upgrading your bathroom is storage. Adequate storage is essential for keeping the space organized and clutter-free. If your bathroom is lacking in storage, there are several solutions to consider. Wall-mounted shelves or cabinets can provide additional storage without taking up valuable floor space. Over-the-toilet shelving units are a great way to utilize vertical space. For a custom look, consider installing built-in niches in the shower or along the walls.

If you have a small bathroom, maximizing storage can be challenging but not impossible. Look for multifunctional furniture, such as a vanity with built-in drawers or a medicine cabinet with adjustable shelves. Hooks and towel bars can also help keep things organized by providing a place to hang towels, robes, and other items. Baskets and bins are useful for corralling smaller items and can add a decorative touch to your bathroom.

Plumbing upgrades can have a significant impact on the functionality of your bathroom. If your bathroom fixtures are outdated or inefficient, consider replacing them with modern, water-saving models. Low-flow toilets, faucets, and showerheads can help reduce water usage without sacrificing performance. Many of these fixtures come with features like dual-flush toilets, which offer different flush options for liquid and solid waste, and aerated showerheads, which mix air with water to maintain pressure while using less water.

For a more extensive upgrade, consider replacing your bathtub or shower. A new bathtub can be a luxurious addition, especially if you opt for a deep

CHAPTER 5: BATHROOM UPGRADES

soaking tub or a whirlpool tub with built-in jets. If space is limited, a walk-in shower with a frameless glass enclosure can make the bathroom feel more open and modern. Consider adding features like built-in benches, handheld showerheads, and multiple spray options for a spa-like experience.

Upgrading your bathroom floor can also enhance both the look and feel of the space. Heated floors are a popular luxury upgrade that adds comfort, especially in colder climates. Electric or hydronic heating systems can be installed under tile, stone, or even vinyl flooring to provide gentle, even heat. This not only makes the bathroom more comfortable but can also help dry out the floor and reduce the risk of mold and mildew.

Ventilation is another important aspect of a functional bathroom. Proper ventilation helps control moisture levels and prevents the growth of mold and mildew. If your bathroom doesn't already have an exhaust fan, installing one can make a big difference. Look for a fan with a timer or humidity sensor to ensure it runs long enough to clear out moisture after showers and baths. If you're replacing an existing fan, choose one with a higher CFM (cubic feet per minute) rating for better airflow.

Accessibility is an important consideration, especially if you plan to age in place or have family members with mobility issues. Simple upgrades like grab bars in the shower or near the toilet can provide added safety and support. A walk-in shower with a low threshold or a roll-in shower with a built-in bench can make bathing easier and safer. Consider installing a handheld showerhead with a long hose for greater flexibility and ease of use.

Finally, let's talk about the finishing touches that can make your bathroom truly special. These small details can add personality and style to your space. Consider adding a few decorative elements, such as artwork, plants, or candles. A stylish shower curtain or new bath linens can also make a big impact. Look for accessories that complement your overall design, and don't be afraid to mix and match textures and colors.

One of the easiest ways to add a touch of luxury to your bathroom is by upgrading your towels and bath mat. Invest in high-quality, plush towels that feel soft and absorbent. Choose a bath mat that is both functional and stylish, providing a non-slip surface while adding a pop of color or pattern. Consider adding a heated towel rack for an extra touch of comfort, especially in the colder months.

Another simple but effective upgrade is to replace your shower curtain or add a glass shower door. A new shower curtain in a bold pattern or elegant fabric can instantly refresh the look of your bathroom. If you prefer a more permanent solution, a glass shower door can make the space feel larger and more open. Frameless glass doors offer a sleek, modern look, while framed doors can add a touch of traditional style.

Don't forget about the importance of scent in creating a relaxing bathroom environment. Consider adding scented candles, essential oil diffusers, or even a small bouquet of fresh flowers. Choose scents that promote relaxation and well-being, such as lavender, eucalyptus, or citrus. These small touches can make your bathroom feel like a spa retreat, providing a calming atmosphere for your daily routine.

In this chapter, we've explored a wide range of bathroom upgrades, from simple cosmetic changes to more extensive renovations. Whether you're updating fixtures, adding new tile, or completely overhauling the space, each improvement can enhance the functionality and aesthetics of your bathroom. By carefully planning your upgrades and paying attention to the details, you can create a bathroom that meets your needs and reflects your personal style. From refreshing the color scheme to adding luxurious touches, there are countless ways to transform your bathroom into a beautiful and functional oasis. So gather your tools, roll up your sleeves, and get ready to tackle your next bathroom project with confidence.

Chapter 6: Outdoor Improvements

Stepping outside, the potential for home improvement doesn't end at the front door. Outdoor spaces offer a canvas for creativity, comfort, and functionality. Whether it's a lush garden, a cozy patio, or a new deck, upgrading your outdoor areas can enhance your living space and increase the value of your home. In this chapter, we'll explore a variety of outdoor improvement projects, from gardening and landscaping to constructing decks and patios. So, grab your sunscreen, and let's get to work on transforming your outdoor space into an inviting extension of your home.

Gardening is one of the most rewarding ways to enhance your outdoor space. Not only does it improve the aesthetic appeal of your yard, but it also provides a peaceful retreat and even fresh produce if you choose to grow vegetables or herbs. Start by assessing your garden's current state. Consider the climate, soil type, and the amount of sunlight your garden receives throughout the day. These factors will influence the types of plants that will thrive in your garden.

Choosing the right plants is crucial for a successful garden. Native plants are always a good choice as they are adapted to the local climate and soil conditions, making them easier to care for. They also support local wildlife, such as bees and butterflies. If you're interested in a low-maintenance garden, consider drought-tolerant plants like succulents or ornamental grasses, which require less water and care.

When planning your garden layout, think about the different zones you want to create. You might want a dedicated area for flowers, a vegetable patch, and perhaps a seating area where you can relax and enjoy your garden. Use a mix of plants with different heights, colors, and textures to create visual interest. Layering plants from tallest at the back to shortest at the front can create depth and make your garden look more dynamic.

Preparing your soil is an essential step in gardening. Healthy soil is the foundation of a thriving garden. Start by testing your soil to determine its pH level and nutrient content. You can buy a soil test kit from a garden center or send a sample to a lab for analysis. Based on the results, you can amend your soil with compost, manure, or other organic matter to improve its fertility and structure.

Planting is both an art and a science. Follow the planting instructions for each type of plant, paying attention to the recommended depth and spacing. Group plants with similar water and light requirements together to make maintenance easier. Mulching around your plants can help retain moisture, suppress weeds, and improve the soil as it decomposes. Water your plants thoroughly after planting and continue to water them regularly, especially during dry spells.

Once your garden is established, ongoing care and maintenance are crucial for keeping it healthy and vibrant. Regularly weed your garden to prevent competition for nutrients and water. Deadhead spent flowers to encourage new blooms and prune shrubs and trees to maintain their shape and health. Fertilize your plants as needed, based on the specific requirements of each type. And don't forget to enjoy the fruits of your labor, whether it's a beautiful bouquet of flowers or a basket of fresh vegetables.

Landscaping goes hand-in-hand with gardening and can significantly enhance the overall look of your outdoor space. Simple landscaping projects, such as adding edging to garden beds, installing a pathway, or creating a focal point with a water feature, can make a big impact. When planning your landscaping, consider the style of your home and choose elements that complement it. A cohesive design will make your outdoor space feel like an extension of your home.

One of the most popular outdoor improvement projects is building a deck. A well-designed deck can provide a versatile space for outdoor dining, entertaining, or simply relaxing. When planning your deck, start by considering the location and size. Choose a spot that offers easy access to your home and provides a good view. The size of your deck should be proportionate to your yard and suit your needs without overwhelming the space.

Selecting the right materials is crucial for a durable and attractive deck. Pressure-treated wood is a common choice due to its affordability and resistance to rot and insects. However, it does require regular maintenance, such as staining and sealing. Composite decking, made from a mix of wood fibers and plastic, is a low-maintenance alternative that offers the look of wood without the upkeep. It's more expensive upfront but can save time and money in the long run. Other options include hardwoods like cedar and redwood, which are naturally resistant to decay, or exotic woods like ipe and teak, which are incredibly durable but also come with a higher price tag.

The construction of your deck begins with the foundation. A solid foundation is critical for a stable and long-lasting deck. You'll need to dig post holes and set the posts in concrete. The spacing of the posts depends on the size and design of your deck, so be sure to follow local building codes and regulations. Once the posts are set, you can install the beams and joists, which form the frame of your deck. Use galvanized or stainless steel fasteners to prevent rust and ensure the structural integrity of your deck.

Laying the decking boards is the next step. Start by securing the first board against the house, ensuring it's straight and level. Leave a small gap between the house and the board for drainage. Continue laying the boards, spacing them evenly to allow for expansion and contraction. Use a drill and screws to secure each board to the joists, or consider hidden fasteners for a cleaner look. Trim any overhanging boards to create a neat edge.

Railings are an important safety feature for your deck and can also add to its aesthetic appeal. Choose a style that complements your deck design, whether it's traditional wooden balusters, sleek metal railings, or even glass panels for an unobstructed view. Secure the railing posts to the deck frame and install the top and bottom rails. Finish by attaching the balusters or panels, ensuring they are evenly spaced and securely fastened.

Once your deck is complete, finish it with a protective sealant or stain to enhance its appearance and protect it from the elements. Regular maintenance, such as cleaning and reapplying sealant, will keep your deck looking great for years to come.

A patio is another great addition to any outdoor space. Patios are typically easier and less expensive to build than decks and can provide a versatile area for outdoor living. When planning your patio, start by choosing the location and size. Consider factors such as sunlight, shade, and proximity to your house. Mark out the area with stakes and string, and measure the dimensions to ensure accuracy.

Selecting the right materials for your patio is essential for durability and aesthetics. Popular options include concrete, pavers, and natural stone. Concrete is affordable and versatile, allowing for various finishes and designs, such as stamped or stained concrete. Pavers, made from brick, concrete, or stone, offer a wide range of colors, shapes, and patterns, making them a flexible choice for creating custom designs. Natural stone, such as flagstone or slate, provides a beautiful and timeless look but can be more expensive and labor-intensive to install.

The first step in building your patio is preparing the ground. Remove any

CHAPTER 6: OUTDOOR IMPROVEMENTS

grass, weeds, or debris from the area, and excavate to a depth of about 6-8 inches, depending on the thickness of your patio material. Lay a layer of gravel or crushed stone to create a stable base, and compact it with a tamper. Add a layer of sand on top, leveling it with a screed board to create a smooth surface for your patio material.

If you're using pavers or stone, start laying them from one corner, working your way out. Use spacers to ensure even gaps between the pavers, and tap them into place with a rubber mallet. Check for level as you go, and adjust the base as needed. Once all the pavers are laid, fill the gaps with sand or polymeric sand, which hardens when wet to help secure the pavers in place. Sweep the sand into the gaps and mist with water to set.

For a concrete patio, you'll need to build a form using wooden boards to contain the concrete. Mix the concrete according to the manufacturer's instructions, and pour it into the form. Use a trowel or float to spread and level the concrete, and create any desired texture or finish. Allow the concrete to cure for several days before removing the form and using the patio.

Adding features like outdoor lighting, furniture, and decor can further enhance your outdoor space. String lights, lanterns, or solar-powered garden lights can create a warm and inviting atmosphere for evening gatherings. Comfortable seating, such as outdoor sofas, chairs, and dining sets, will encourage relaxation and socializing. Decorative elements, such as rugs, cushions, and planters, can add color and personality to your patio or deck.

For those who enjoy cooking and entertaining, an outdoor kitchen or grill area can be a fantastic addition. A simple setup might include a grill, a prep table, and some storage for utensils and supplies. For a more elaborate outdoor kitchen, consider adding features like a sink, refrigerator, and built-in cabinetry. Ensure that any appliances and fixtures are designed for outdoor use and are properly installed to withstand the elements.

Water features, such as fountains, ponds, or waterfalls, can add a soothing and tranquil element to your outdoor space. The sound of running water can create a calming atmosphere and mask unwanted noise from nearby streets or neighbors. When planning a water feature, consider the size and scale of your yard, as well as the maintenance required to keep it clean and functioning.

In this chapter, we've explored a variety of outdoor improvement projects, from gardening and landscaping to building decks and patios. Each project offers unique opportunities to enhance your outdoor space and create a welcoming environment for relaxation and entertainment. By carefully planning and executing your upgrades, you can transform your yard into a beautiful and functional extension of your home. Whether you're a seasoned DIYer or just starting out, there's an outdoor project that's perfect for you. So grab your tools, roll up your sleeves, and get ready to enjoy your new and improved outdoor oasis.

Chapter 7: Energy Efficiency and Insulation

In an era where energy conservation is becoming increasingly important, upgrading your home's energy efficiency is a smart and impactful home improvement project. Not only does it help reduce your carbon footprint, but it also translates into significant cost savings on your utility bills. In this chapter, we'll delve into various methods to improve your home's energy efficiency, focusing on insulation, windows, doors, and renewable energy options. With practical tips and detailed explanations, you'll be well-equipped to make your home more energy-efficient and comfortable.

Let's start with insulation, the unsung hero of energy efficiency. Proper insulation is crucial for maintaining a consistent indoor temperature, reducing the need for heating and cooling. There are several types of insulation, each with its own advantages and applications. The most common types include fiberglass, cellulose, spray foam, and rigid foam board.

Fiberglass insulation is perhaps the most familiar. It's made of fine glass fibers and is available in batts or rolls, which makes it easy to install in walls, attics, and floors. Fiberglass is relatively inexpensive and effective, but it's important to handle it with care as the tiny fibers can irritate your skin and lungs. Always wear gloves, a mask, and protective clothing when working with fiberglass insulation.

Cellulose insulation, made from recycled paper products, is an eco-friendly option. It's treated with fire retardants and can be blown into walls, attics, and other cavities, providing excellent coverage and reducing air leaks. Cellulose is also effective at reducing noise, making it a great choice for soundproofing. However, installation typically requires specialized equipment, so you may need to hire a professional.

Spray foam insulation is a versatile and highly effective option. It expands upon application, filling gaps and creating an airtight seal. This makes it ideal for hard-to-reach areas and irregular spaces. There are two types of spray foam: open-cell and closed-cell. Open-cell foam is less dense and offers soundproofing benefits, while closed-cell foam is denser and provides a higher R-value (a measure of insulation's effectiveness). Spray foam tends to be more expensive, but its superior performance can justify the cost.

Rigid foam board insulation is made from materials like polystyrene, polyisocyanurate, and polyurethane. These boards provide a high R-value and are commonly used in exterior walls, roofs, and foundations. They are particularly useful in areas where space is limited but high insulation value is needed. Installation is straightforward, involving cutting the boards to size and securing them with adhesive or fasteners.

Properly insulating your attic is one of the most effective ways to improve your home's energy efficiency. Heat rises, so a poorly insulated attic can be a major source of heat loss in the winter and heat gain in the summer. Start by sealing any gaps or cracks where air might escape, such as around chimneys, vents, and wiring. Next, lay down a vapor barrier to prevent moisture from entering the insulation. Then, install your chosen insulation material, ensuring it covers the entire attic floor and extends to the edges without gaps.

Walls are another critical area for insulation. If your home's walls are uninsulated or poorly insulated, they can be a significant source of heat loss. For existing homes, blown-in cellulose or spray foam insulation is often the best solution, as these materials can be installed without removing drywall.

CHAPTER 7: ENERGY EFFICIENCY AND INSULATION

For new construction or major renovations, consider using batt insulation or rigid foam boards to achieve the desired R-value.

Don't forget about floors and basements. Insulating these areas can prevent heat loss and make your home more comfortable. For floors above unheated spaces, such as garages or crawl spaces, fiberglass batts can be installed between the floor joists. Basements can be insulated with rigid foam boards or spray foam to create a continuous barrier against cold and moisture.

Windows and doors are common culprits for energy loss. Upgrading to energy-efficient windows and doors can make a significant difference in your home's overall efficiency. Look for products with low U-values (indicating better insulating properties) and low emissivity (low-E) coatings, which reflect heat and reduce thermal transfer. Double or triple-pane windows with gas fills, such as argon or krypton, offer superior insulation compared to single-pane windows.

When replacing windows, proper installation is key to ensuring they perform as expected. Make sure the windows are level, square, and securely fastened. Use expanding foam insulation around the frame to seal any gaps and prevent drafts. Installing weatherstripping and caulking around the edges can further improve efficiency.

Doors can also be a source of drafts and energy loss. Solid wood or metal doors with foam insulation cores provide better thermal performance than hollow-core doors. Install weatherstripping around the door frame to seal gaps, and use a door sweep at the bottom to prevent drafts. If your door has a window, consider upgrading to a double-pane or low-E glass for better insulation.

Renewable energy options, such as solar panels and wind turbines, can significantly reduce your reliance on traditional energy sources and lower your utility bills. Solar panels are the most common and accessible renewable energy option for homeowners. They convert sunlight into electricity and can be installed on your roof or in your yard. The initial investment can be high, but many governments offer incentives and rebates to offset the cost. Over time, the savings on your energy bills can make solar panels a worthwhile investment.

When considering solar panels, evaluate your home's solar potential. Factors like roof orientation, angle, and shading from trees or other structures will affect how much sunlight your panels can capture. A south-facing roof with minimal shading is ideal, but east or west-facing roofs can also work well. Consult with a professional installer to determine the best placement and configuration for your system.

Wind turbines are another renewable energy option, though they are less common for residential use due to zoning regulations and space requirements. Small wind turbines can be installed on properties with sufficient wind resources and open space. Like solar panels, wind turbines can reduce your dependence on grid electricity and lower your energy bills. However, they require more maintenance and have a longer payback period compared to solar panels.

In addition to generating your own renewable energy, you can improve your home's efficiency by upgrading to energy-efficient appliances and lighting. Look for appliances with the ENERGY STAR label, which indicates they meet strict energy efficiency guidelines. Replacing old, inefficient appliances with ENERGY STAR-rated models can save a significant amount of energy and money over time.

Lighting accounts for a substantial portion of your home's energy use. Switching to energy-efficient lighting, such as LED bulbs, can drastically reduce your electricity consumption. LED bulbs use up to 80% less energy than traditional incandescent bulbs and last much longer. They are available in a variety of colors and brightness levels, making them suitable for any room in your home.

CHAPTER 7: ENERGY EFFICIENCY AND INSULATION

Smart home technology can also play a role in improving energy efficiency. Smart thermostats, for example, allow you to control your home's heating and cooling remotely via a smartphone app. They can learn your schedule and adjust the temperature automatically to maximize comfort and efficiency. Some models even provide energy usage reports and tips for saving energy.

Smart lighting systems can be programmed to turn off when not in use or dim during certain times of the day to save energy. Smart plugs and power strips can help reduce standby power consumption by cutting off power to devices that are not in use. By integrating these technologies into your home, you can take greater control of your energy usage and identify areas where you can make further improvements.

Water heating is another area where energy efficiency can be improved. Traditional water heaters constantly heat and store water, leading to significant energy loss. Tankless water heaters, also known as on-demand water heaters, heat water only when needed, reducing energy consumption. They are more efficient and take up less space but can be more expensive to install. Heat pump water heaters are another efficient option, using electricity to move heat from the air or ground to heat water. These units can be up to three times more efficient than traditional water heaters.

Improving your home's energy efficiency is a multifaceted endeavor that involves a combination of insulation, upgrading windows and doors, incorporating renewable energy sources, and adopting energy-efficient appliances and smart home technology. Each improvement contributes to a more comfortable, sustainable, and cost-effective living environment. As you implement these changes, you'll not only enjoy the immediate benefits of lower utility bills and increased comfort, but you'll also be making a positive impact on the environment.

In this chapter, we've covered a range of strategies to enhance your home's energy efficiency, from proper insulation techniques to the adoption of renewable energy sources. By taking a comprehensive approach to energy efficiency, you can create a home that is both eco-friendly and economical. Whether you're starting with small upgrades or planning a major renovation, each step brings you closer to a more energy-efficient and sustainable home. So, gear up, and let's make your home a model of energy efficiency and comfort.

Chapter 8: Electrical and Lighting Projects

Electrical and lighting projects can seem intimidating at first, but with the right knowledge and precautions, many of these tasks are well within the reach of the average DIYer. Upgrading your home's electrical system and lighting not only enhances functionality and safety but can also significantly improve your home's aesthetic appeal. In this chapter, we'll cover basic electrical safety, essential tools, and techniques for common electrical projects, as well as tips for enhancing your home's lighting.

Electrical Safety: Before diving into any electrical project, it's crucial to understand and prioritize safety. Electricity is powerful and can be dangerous if not handled correctly. Always turn off the power at the circuit breaker before starting any electrical work. Double-check that the power is off using a voltage tester or a non-contact voltage detector. These tools are inexpensive and can save your life.

Wear rubber-soled shoes and use insulated tools to reduce the risk of electric shock. Avoid working with electrical systems in wet or damp conditions, and make sure your workspace is well-lit and free of clutter. If you're ever unsure about a project or encounter something beyond your skill level, don't hesitate to call a licensed electrician.

Essential Tools: Having the right tools is essential for any electrical project. Some basic tools you'll need include a voltage tester, wire strippers, needle-nose pliers, a screwdriver set, a utility knife, electrical tape, and a circuit tester. Wire nuts and electrical connectors are also useful for connecting wires safely and securely. A fish tape or wire puller can help when you need to run wires through walls or conduits.

Switches and Outlets: Upgrading switches and outlets is a relatively simple project that can make a big difference in your home's functionality and appearance. Start by choosing the right type of switch or outlet for your needs. Standard single-pole switches control a single light or fixture from one location. Three-way and four-way switches allow you to control a light from two or more locations, such as at the top and bottom of a staircase.

Replacing a switch or outlet involves turning off the power, removing the cover plate, and unscrewing the switch or outlet from the electrical box. Carefully pull the device out of the box, taking note of how the wires are connected. Most switches and outlets have screw terminals for attaching wires. Loosen the screws, disconnect the wires, and remove the old device. Attach the wires to the new switch or outlet, ensuring they are connected to the correct terminals. Tighten the screws, tuck the wires back into the box, and secure the new device in place. Finally, replace the cover plate and turn the power back on.

Installing a Ceiling Fan: A ceiling fan can improve air circulation and add a stylish touch to a room. Installing one involves similar steps to installing a light fixture, with a few additional considerations. First, ensure that the electrical box in your ceiling is rated to support the weight of a ceiling fan. If it's not, you'll need to replace it with a fan-rated box.

Turn off the power and remove any existing light fixture. Follow the manufacturer's instructions to assemble the fan, and mount the bracket to the electrical box. Connect the wires according to the instructions, usually matching black to black, white to white, and green or bare copper to the ground wire. Secure the fan to the bracket, attach the blades, and install any light kit if included. Turn the power back on and test the fan to ensure it operates correctly.

CHAPTER 8: ELECTRICAL AND LIGHTING PROJECTS

Lighting Projects: Updating your home's lighting can transform the look and feel of your space. Whether you're adding new fixtures, upgrading existing ones, or incorporating smart lighting technology, there are plenty of options to explore.

Recessed Lighting: Recessed lights, also known as can lights or downlights, are installed into the ceiling and provide a sleek, modern look. They're great for general lighting, task lighting, and accent lighting. Installing recessed lighting involves cutting holes in the ceiling, running electrical wiring, and securing the light fixtures in place.

Start by planning the layout of your recessed lights, ensuring they are evenly spaced and provide adequate illumination for the room. Turn off the power and use a stud finder to locate joists and other obstacles in the ceiling. Cut holes for the lights using a hole saw or drywall saw, and run electrical wiring from the power source to each light location. Connect the wiring to the light fixtures, secure them in place, and install the trim. Finally, turn the power back on and test the lights.

Pendant Lights: Pendant lights are versatile fixtures that can add style and focused lighting to kitchens, dining areas, and other spaces. They hang from the ceiling by a cord, chain, or rod, and come in various designs to suit any decor. Installing a pendant light is similar to installing a ceiling fan or recessed light.

Start by turning off the power and removing any existing fixture. Assemble the pendant light according to the manufacturer's instructions, and install the mounting bracket to the electrical box. Connect the wires, matching black to black, white to white, and green or bare copper to the ground wire. Secure the pendant light to the bracket, adjust the length of the cord or chain as needed, and install the bulb and shade. Turn the power back on and test the light.

Under-Cabinet Lighting: Under-cabinet lighting is a great way to add task lighting to your kitchen or workspace. It illuminates countertops and work surfaces, making it easier to see what you're doing. There are several types of under-cabinet lighting, including LED strips, puck lights, and fluorescent fixtures.

Installing under-cabinet lighting typically involves mounting the lights to the underside of your cabinets and connecting them to a power source. LED strips are a popular choice because they are low-profile, energy-efficient, and easy to install. Measure and cut the LED strips to fit under your cabinets, peel off the adhesive backing, and stick the strips in place. Connect the strips to a power supply and plug it into an outlet or hardwire it to a switch.

Smart Lighting: Smart lighting systems allow you to control your lights remotely using a smartphone app, voice commands, or automation. They can enhance convenience, energy efficiency, and security. Smart bulbs are the easiest way to get started with smart lighting. Simply replace your existing bulbs with smart bulbs, and use the manufacturer's app to connect them to your home's Wi-Fi network.

For more advanced smart lighting systems, consider smart switches, dimmers, and hubs. Smart switches replace your existing light switches and allow you to control your lights remotely. Smart dimmers let you adjust the brightness of your lights, and smart hubs can integrate multiple devices for centralized control. Installation typically involves replacing your existing switches with smart switches, following the same steps as for standard switches.

Outdoor Lighting: Outdoor lighting can enhance the safety, security, and beauty of your home's exterior. There are many options for outdoor lighting, including pathway lights, wall-mounted lights, floodlights, and landscape lighting.

Pathway lights are ideal for illuminating walkways and driveways, making it easier to navigate your yard at night. Solar-powered pathway lights are

CHAPTER 8: ELECTRICAL AND LIGHTING PROJECTS

easy to install and require no wiring. Simply place them along your path, and they'll charge during the day and light up at night.

Wall-mounted lights, such as sconces or lanterns, can add style and illumination to your home's exterior. They're typically installed near entryways or along the walls of your house. Installing a wall-mounted light involves mounting the fixture to the wall and connecting it to the existing wiring.

Floodlights provide bright, focused illumination and are often used for security purposes. Motion-sensor floodlights can deter intruders and alert you to movement around your home. Installing a floodlight involves mounting the fixture to the wall or eaves and connecting it to the wiring.

Landscape lighting can highlight the features of your yard, such as trees, shrubs, and architectural elements. Low-voltage landscape lighting systems are easy to install and safe to use. They typically consist of a transformer, low-voltage wiring, and various light fixtures. Place the fixtures where desired, run the wiring, and connect it to the transformer. Plug the transformer into an outdoor outlet, and adjust the lights as needed.

Incorporating Dimmers: Installing dimmer switches can enhance the versatility and ambiance of your lighting. Dimmers allow you to adjust the brightness of your lights, creating the perfect mood for any occasion. They're particularly useful in living rooms, dining rooms, and bedrooms.

To install a dimmer switch, start by turning off the power and removing the existing switch. Connect the wires to the dimmer switch, following the manufacturer's instructions. Typically, this involves connecting the black wire from the wall to the black wire on the dimmer, the white wire to the white wire, and the ground wire to the green wire. Secure the dimmer switch to the electrical box, replace the cover plate, and turn the power back on. Test the dimmer to ensure it operates correctly.

Childproofing Electrical Outlets: If you have young children, childproofing your electrical outlets is essential for their safety. Tamper-resistant outlets, also known as childproof outlets, have built-in shutters that prevent foreign objects from being inserted. These outlets are a simple and effective way to childproof your home.

To install tamper-resistant outlets, turn off the power and remove the existing outlets. Connect the wires to the new tamper-resistant outlets, following the same steps as for standard outlets. Secure the outlets to the electrical box, replace the cover plates, and turn the power back on. Test the outlets to ensure they work properly.

Electrical and lighting projects can significantly enhance your home's functionality, safety, and aesthetics. By following proper safety precautions, using the right tools, and understanding the basics of electrical work, you can successfully complete a variety of projects. Whether you're upgrading switches and outlets, installing new light fixtures, or incorporating smart lighting technology, each project brings you one step closer to a more comfortable and efficient home. So, roll up your sleeves, grab your tools, and let's illuminate your home with these electrical and lighting improvements.

Chapter 9: Furniture and Woodworking

There's something deeply satisfying about creating furniture with your own hands. Woodworking not only allows you to customize your home's decor to perfectly suit your tastes and needs, but it also offers a rewarding hobby that combines creativity with craftsmanship. This chapter delves into the world of furniture building and woodworking, covering everything from basic tools and techniques to detailed projects. Whether you're a beginner or an experienced woodworker, you'll find plenty of inspiration and guidance here.

Starting with the Basics: To embark on your woodworking journey, you'll need some essential tools. While it's tempting to buy every shiny new tool in the store, you can accomplish a lot with a few basics. A good tape measure is indispensable for accurate measurements, while a combination square is useful for marking and checking 90-degree angles. A handsaw is perfect for making precise cuts without the need for power tools, and a set of chisels will come in handy for fine detail work and joinery. Clamps are essential for holding pieces together while glue dries, and a classic hammer is necessary for driving nails and other fasteners. Both Phillips and flathead screwdrivers are needed for assembling furniture, and a cordless drill with a variety of bits will make many tasks easier. Finally, a sanding block or power sander smooths out rough edges and surfaces for a polished finish.

Once you've gathered your tools, it's important to learn the basics of woodworking safety. Always wear safety glasses to protect your eyes from flying debris, and use ear protection when working with loud power tools. Keep your work area clean and free of clutter to prevent accidents, and never rush through a project. Taking your time ensures both safety and precision.

Choosing the right type of wood is crucial for the success of your project. Hardwoods, such as oak, maple, and cherry, are durable and often used for furniture that needs to withstand heavy use. Softwoods, like pine and cedar, are easier to work with and can be a good choice for beginners or projects that don't require as much strength. Consider the grain and color of the wood as well. Hardwoods typically have a more pronounced grain and a richer color, making them ideal for pieces where aesthetics are important. Softwoods usually have a simpler grain and a lighter color, which can be stained or painted to match your desired look.

The way pieces of wood are joined together can significantly impact the strength and appearance of your furniture. The simplest type of joint is the butt joint, where two pieces of wood are joined end to end. It's not the strongest joint, but it's easy to make and can be reinforced with screws or dowels. A dado joint is a slot cut into one piece of wood that another piece fits into, often used for shelves and drawer bottoms. Mortise and tenon is a strong, classic joint where a protruding tenon fits into a mortise hole, ideal for frames and furniture legs. The dovetail joint is known for its strength and decorative appearance and is often used in drawer construction. Lastly, the rabbet joint is a groove cut along the edge of a board, often used for the back panels of cabinets. Mastering these joinery techniques will significantly expand your woodworking capabilities and allow you to create stronger, more durable furniture.

Now that you've got the basics down, let's dive into some woodworking projects. A simple bookshelf is a great beginner project. It involves basic cuts and joinery, and you can customize it to fit your space perfectly. Use dado joints to secure the shelves and add a back panel with rabbet joints for extra stability. A coffee table can be as simple or complex as you like. For a basic version, use a solid piece of wood for the top and add four legs with mortise and tenon joints. Sand it smooth and finish with a stain or paint. Building a dining table is more advanced but incredibly rewarding. Use sturdy hardwood for the top and legs, and join them with mortise and tenon joints. Add an apron (a frame beneath the tabletop) for extra support. The classic Adirondack chair is comfortable and stylish. It involves cutting multiple slats for the back and seat, which are then attached to a sturdy frame. Use weather-resistant wood like cedar or treated pine for durability.

Let's walk through the process of building a simple bookshelf. This project is perfect for beginners and provides a solid foundation for more complex projects. To start, gather your materials and tools. You'll need plywood or solid wood for the shelves and sides, a back panel (plywood), wood glue, screws, sandpaper, stain or paint, a tape measure, combination square, handsaw or circular saw, drill, and clamps.

Decide on the dimensions of your bookshelf. A standard size might be 30 inches wide, 12 inches deep, and 48 inches tall. Plan the spacing of the shelves; for example, you could have four shelves with approximately 12 inches of height between each. Cut the sides, shelves, and top/bottom pieces to size. For a 48-inch tall bookshelf, cut two side pieces 48 inches long, and five shelf pieces 30 inches long (four shelves plus the top). Cut the back panel to fit the overall dimensions of the bookshelf, approximately 30 inches by 48 inches.

Mark the locations for the shelves on the inside of the side pieces. Use a combination square to ensure the lines are straight and even. Apply wood glue to the ends of the shelves and fit them into place on one side piece. Use clamps to hold them in position, then drill pilot holes and insert screws to secure the shelves. Repeat the process for the other side piece.

Apply wood glue to the top and bottom pieces and fit them into place between the side pieces. Secure them with screws. Apply wood glue along the edges of the back panel and place it on the back of the bookshelf. Secure it with screws, ensuring it's flush with the edges. Sand all surfaces and edges to remove any rough spots and prepare the wood for finishing. Apply your choice of stain or paint, following the manufacturer's instructions. Allow it to dry completely before using the bookshelf.

As you gain confidence and experience, you can explore more advanced woodworking techniques and projects. Adding decorative inlays or veneers can enhance the beauty of your furniture. Inlays involve embedding contrasting materials, like wood or metal, into the surface of your piece. Veneers are thin slices of wood applied to the surface, often used to create intricate patterns. Bending wood can create elegant curves and shapes in your furniture. This technique involves soaking or steaming the wood to make it pliable, then clamping it into a form until it dries and retains the new shape. Wood carving and turning add intricate details and designs to your projects. Carving involves using chisels and gouges to remove material and create patterns or images. Turning involves mounting wood on a lathe and shaping it with various tools to create symmetrical objects like bowls, spindles, and legs.

Proper care and maintenance of your tools will ensure they last longer and perform better. Keep your blades and bits sharp, clean your tools after each use, and store them in a dry, organized space. Regularly check for wear and tear, and replace any damaged or worn parts. Woodworking is a journey of continuous learning and improvement. Each project you undertake will build your skills and expand your creativity. From simple shelves to intricate furniture, the possibilities are endless. The satisfaction of creating something beautiful and functional with your own hands is unmatched. So gather your tools, choose your project, and start building a piece that you can be proud of.

Chapter 10: Home Maintenance and Repairs

Keeping a house in good shape requires regular maintenance and the occasional repair job. While some tasks are best left to professionals, there are many things you can handle on your own. This chapter will guide you through essential home maintenance and repair tasks, helping you keep your home in tip-top condition.

One of the most important aspects of home maintenance is regular inspections. Checking various parts of your home periodically can help you catch problems early, before they become more serious and costly. Start with your roof, as it is your home's first line of defense against the elements. Look for missing, damaged, or curling shingles. Check for signs of leaks, such as water stains on your ceilings or walls. Clean your gutters and downspouts to ensure water can flow freely, preventing damage to your roof and foundation.

Windows and doors are other critical areas to inspect. Look for drafts, which can indicate worn or damaged weatherstripping. Replacing weatherstripping is a simple yet effective way to improve energy efficiency and comfort in your home. Check for cracks or gaps in the caulking around windows and doors, and reapply caulk as needed to maintain a good seal.

Your home's HVAC system also requires regular attention. Change the filters in your furnace and air conditioner every three months, or more frequently if you have pets or allergies. Clean the coils on your air conditioner and ensure the outdoor unit is free of debris. Schedule professional maintenance for your HVAC system at least once a year to keep it running efficiently and to extend its lifespan.

Plumbing is another area where regular maintenance can prevent costly repairs. Check for leaks under sinks and around toilets, as well as in your basement or crawl space. Small leaks can often be fixed with pipe tape or sealant, but larger issues may require a professional plumber. Clean your drains regularly with a mixture of baking soda and vinegar to prevent clogs. If you notice slow draining or gurgling noises, it might be time to snake the drain or use a plunger to clear the blockage.

Maintaining your home's electrical system is crucial for safety. Periodically inspect your electrical panel for signs of wear or corrosion. Ensure that all circuit breakers are functioning properly and that there are no loose wires. Test your smoke detectors and carbon monoxide detectors monthly, and replace the batteries at least once a year. If you notice flickering lights, frequent breaker trips, or outlets that are warm to the touch, it's time to call a licensed electrician.

Exterior maintenance is equally important. Inspect your home's siding for damage, such as cracks, holes, or peeling paint. Repair any issues promptly to prevent moisture from entering and causing further damage. Power wash your siding, deck, and driveway annually to remove dirt, mildew, and grime. Check your foundation for cracks or signs of settling, and address any issues with a professional if needed.

One of the more satisfying maintenance tasks is taking care of your lawn and garden. Regular mowing, trimming, and watering can keep your yard looking its best. Fertilize your lawn in the spring and fall, and aerate it once a year to promote healthy growth. Prune shrubs and trees to remove dead or damaged

CHAPTER 10: HOME MAINTENANCE AND REPAIRS

branches and to encourage new growth. Mulch your flower beds to retain moisture and suppress weeds.

Indoor maintenance tasks often revolve around keeping your home clean and functional. Vacuum and dust regularly to reduce allergens and keep your living spaces comfortable. Clean your carpets and upholstery annually to remove deep-seated dirt and stains. Wipe down your kitchen cabinets and appliances to keep them looking fresh and to prevent the buildup of grease and grime.

Maintaining your home's interior also involves checking for signs of wear and tear. Inspect your walls and ceilings for cracks or holes, and patch them as needed. Repaint walls every few years to keep your home looking vibrant and to protect the surfaces from damage. Check your floors for scratches, dents, or loose boards, and repair or replace them as necessary.

Now, let's delve into some common repair tasks that you can handle on your own. One of the most frequent issues homeowners face is a leaky faucet. Fixing a leaky faucet not only saves water but also prevents potential water damage. Start by turning off the water supply to the faucet. Disassemble the faucet handle to access the valve. Depending on the type of faucet, you may need to replace a washer, a cartridge, or a valve seat. Reassemble the faucet and turn the water back on to check for leaks.

Another common problem is a running toilet. This can waste a significant amount of water and increase your utility bills. The most common cause of a running toilet is a faulty flapper valve. To fix it, turn off the water supply to the toilet and flush to empty the tank. Remove the old flapper valve and replace it with a new one, making sure it creates a proper seal. Turn the water back on and test the toilet to ensure it's working correctly.

Clogged drains are another issue many homeowners encounter. A plunger is often the first tool to try when dealing with a clog. For tougher clogs, a plumbing snake can be used to reach further into the pipe and break up the blockage. Chemical drain cleaners can also be effective, but use them sparingly as they can damage your pipes over time. For recurring clogs, it might be worth installing a drain strainer to catch hair and debris before they go down the drain.

Patching drywall is a skill that every homeowner should learn. Whether it's from moving furniture or an accidental bump, holes in drywall are common. Start by cleaning the area around the hole. For small holes, use a patch kit that includes a mesh patch and joint compound. Apply the patch over the hole, then spread a thin layer of joint compound over it, feathering the edges. Allow it to dry, then sand it smooth and apply another coat if needed. For larger holes, you'll need to cut a piece of drywall to fit the hole, secure it with screws, and then tape and mud the seams.

Sometimes, doors and windows can become misaligned, making them difficult to open or close. This is often due to settling or changes in humidity. To fix a sticking door, check the hinges first. Tighten any loose screws and adjust the hinge position if necessary. If the door is still sticking, you may need to plane the edge slightly to ensure a proper fit. For windows, check that the tracks are clean and free of debris. Lubricate the tracks with a silicone spray to improve movement.

Heating and cooling systems are essential for maintaining a comfortable home environment. Regularly replacing air filters is one of the simplest and most effective ways to keep your HVAC system running efficiently. Filters should be replaced every one to three months, depending on the type of filter and the presence of pets or allergies. Additionally, check the area around your outdoor unit to ensure it is free of leaves, grass, and other debris that could obstruct airflow.

Water heaters are another critical component of your home's comfort. Over time, sediment can build up in the tank, reducing efficiency and potentially causing damage. Flushing your water heater annually can help maintain its

CHAPTER 10: HOME MAINTENANCE AND REPAIRS

performance. Turn off the power or gas supply to the heater, attach a garden hose to the drain valve, and direct the hose to a safe drainage area. Open the valve and allow the tank to empty, then close the valve, remove the hose, and refill the tank. Turn the power or gas supply back on and check for proper operation.

Maintaining your home's appliances can extend their lifespan and improve efficiency. Clean your refrigerator coils every six months to prevent dust buildup that can cause the motor to overheat. Check the seals on your refrigerator and freezer doors to ensure they are tight and free of cracks. Clean the lint filter in your dryer after every use, and periodically check the dryer vent for blockages to prevent fires and improve drying efficiency.

Another key aspect of home maintenance is pest control. Regularly inspect your home for signs of pests, such as droppings, gnaw marks, or nesting materials. Seal any gaps or cracks in your home's exterior to prevent pests from entering. Keep food stored in airtight containers and maintain a clean home to reduce the risk of infestations. If you encounter a persistent pest problem, consider hiring a professional exterminator.

Maintaining your home is an ongoing process that requires regular attention and care. By staying on top of these tasks, you can prevent small issues from becoming major problems, save money on repairs, and keep your home safe, comfortable, and looking its best. Whether you're fixing a leaky faucet, patching drywall, or maintaining your HVAC system, each task you complete contributes to the overall health and longevity of your home. So, take pride in your home maintenance efforts and enjoy the peace of mind that comes with a well-cared-for home.

Conclusion

As we come to the end of our journey through the world of DIY home improvement, it's clear that taking matters into your own hands can be both immensely rewarding and occasionally frustrating. Whether you've been fixing a leaky faucet, painting a room, or building custom furniture, each project has its unique challenges and triumphs. But one thing remains constant: the satisfaction of improving your home with your own efforts.

Home improvement is about more than just making your living space look better. It's about creating an environment that reflects your personality, meets your needs, and enhances your daily life. Each project, big or small, contributes to a more comfortable, functional, and enjoyable home. From the moment you decide to start a project to the final touches, the process of transforming your space is a journey of creativity, learning, and sometimes even a bit of trial and error.

Let's take a moment to reflect on some of the key aspects we've covered, starting with the fundamental importance of preparation. Proper planning and preparation are the cornerstones of any successful DIY project. Before diving into a project, taking the time to assess your needs, set realistic goals, and gather all necessary tools and materials can save you a lot of headaches down the road. A well-thought-out plan can make even the most complex tasks manageable and ensure that you stay on track and within budget.

CONCLUSION

We delved into the basics of painting and wallpapering, discovering that these tasks, while seemingly straightforward, require careful attention to detail. The right paint or wallpaper can dramatically change the look and feel of a room. From selecting the perfect color and texture to mastering the techniques of application, every step contributes to the final result. It's about more than just slapping on a new coat; it's about understanding how color and design elements work together to create a harmonious space.

Flooring projects, too, demand precision and patience. Whether you're laying hardwood, tile, or laminate, each type of flooring brings its own set of requirements and challenges. The right flooring not only enhances the aesthetics of your home but also its functionality. Proper installation ensures durability and longevity, making your floors a worthwhile investment that stands the test of time.

When we ventured into the kitchen and bathroom remodels, we encountered projects that significantly impact both the value and enjoyment of your home. These spaces are essential to daily life, and upgrading them can improve efficiency and comfort. From planning the layout and selecting materials to installing cabinets, countertops, and fixtures, each decision shapes the functionality and style of these critical areas.

Outdoor improvements brought us into the realm of gardens, patios, and decks. Enhancing your outdoor space can extend your living area and create a relaxing retreat right in your backyard. Gardening requires knowledge of plants, soil, and climate, while building structures like decks and patios involves understanding construction techniques and materials. These projects connect you with nature and provide a space for leisure and entertainment.

Energy efficiency and insulation projects reminded us of the importance of creating a sustainable and cost-effective home. Improving insulation, upgrading windows and doors, and incorporating renewable energy sources like solar panels can significantly reduce your energy consumption and utility bills. These improvements not only benefit the environment but also enhance the comfort of your home by maintaining consistent temperatures and reducing drafts.

Electrical and lighting projects highlighted the impact of proper lighting on the ambiance and functionality of your home. From installing new fixtures and outlets to upgrading to smart lighting systems, these projects can transform your living spaces. Understanding basic electrical safety and techniques is crucial for successfully completing these tasks and ensuring the safety of your home.

Furniture building and woodworking projects allowed us to explore the creative side of DIY. Crafting custom furniture pieces not only provides functional items tailored to your needs but also offers a sense of accomplishment and pride. Learning different joinery techniques, working with various types of wood, and mastering the use of woodworking tools open up endless possibilities for creating unique and beautiful furniture.

Home maintenance and repairs are ongoing responsibilities that ensure your home remains in good condition. Regular inspections, timely repairs, and preventive maintenance can prevent minor issues from becoming major problems. From fixing leaky faucets and running toilets to maintaining HVAC systems and cleaning gutters, these tasks are essential for the longevity and safety of your home.

Throughout our exploration, the theme of self-reliance and empowerment has been a constant thread. Taking on DIY projects not only saves money but also builds valuable skills and confidence. Each project completed is a testament to your ability to improve and maintain your home, creating a living space that truly reflects your style and needs.

The world of DIY home improvement is vast and varied, offering endless opportunities for creativity and growth. While not every project may go smoothly, and mistakes are inevitable, each challenge is an opportunity to learn and improve. The key is to approach each task with patience, curiosity, and a willingness to learn.

As you continue on your home improvement journey, remember that every project, no matter how small, contributes to the overall well-being and functionality of your home. It's about more than just the physical changes; it's about creating a space where you feel comfortable, happy, and proud. Whether you're tackling a major renovation or simply updating a room with a fresh coat of paint, each step brings you closer to a home that reflects your unique personality and lifestyle.

In the end, home improvement is a labor of love. It's about investing time, effort, and creativity into the place where you live, laugh, and create memories. So keep those tools handy, stay curious, and continue to explore the endless possibilities that DIY home improvement has to offer.

Made in the USA
Columbia, SC
01 May 2025